THE SPIDER WEB

LOBNA E. ATALLAH

Austin Macauley Publishers™
LONDON · CAMBRIDGE · NEW YORK · SHARJAH

Copyright © Lubna E. Atallah 2024

The right of **Lubna E. Atallah** to be identified as author of this work has been asserted by the author in accordance with Federal Law No. (7) of UAE, Year 2002, Concerning Copyrights and Neighboring Rights.

All rights reserved. No part of this publication may be reproduced, stored in a retrieval system, or transmitted in any form or by any means, electronic, mechanical, photocopying, recording, or otherwise, without the prior permission of the publishers.

Any person who commits any unauthorized act in relation to this publication may be liable to legal prosecution and civil claims for damages.

The age group that matches the content of the books has been classified according to the age classification system issued by the Ministry of Culture and Youth.

ISBN - 9789948776406 - (Paperback)
ISBN - 9789948776413 - (E-book)

Application Number: MC-10-01-7019286
Age Classification: E

Printer Name: iPrint Global Ltd
Printer Address: Witchford, England

First Published 2024
AUSTIN MACAULEY PUBLISHERS FZE
Sharjah Publishing City
P.O. Box [519201]
Sharjah, UAE
www.austinmacauley.ae
+971 655 95 202

To my partner in rhyme
My "discoverer" back in the time

To my heart's eternal champ
Thank you for the magic lamp

To all my supporters, from the heart
I dedicate this humble piece of art.

MY MIS-ERY

Mis-understood
Mis-judged
Mis-heard
Mis-loved
Mis-read
Mis-placed
Mis-led by your mis-trust
But to you
I'll always be a mis-merizing mis-tery.

LOSS

When I lost you, I lost a big part of myself
I put my heart on a shelf
And later on could not reach for it.
You left me heartless, soulless, barely alive
All I did was to survive
And I was not good at it.
Now, with you haunting my every dream
Triggering every scream
I float
As I got nothing I sought
Only to myself I brought
More misery.
One word is all I want to say
I want to express it in every way.
One word is all my ears crave—
One word is all it takes to save
me. Put your ego aside
And in this confide:
I have stripped off all reasons to accept a shrug.
Your "no" will simply pull my plug.

DEMONS

Knocking on my memories, so strong
An outsider that does not belong
Alarmed, my senses go astray
And no more do I feel like a needle in the hay
Only when I thought my demons were gone
He turned into the worst one
Having lived in the shadow all these years
Truly embracing my fears
A terrible dread runs through my veins
Terrorizing all that—relatively—seems sane
And that ferocious notion
Strikes my every rational emotion
I go on hands and knees
Cutting my way through melancholy
But, the demon that he is, breaks his chains
Unleashing a fury not even hell can contain
And with a 'tick' never followed by a 'tock'
My whole being gets suck
Into a dimension I've never been
To open my eyes to virtuous sin
With no one harmed, it never was
So stated by agony's laws
And I see humans go on, and here I am
Standing at the edge of the abyss,
Not giving a damn!

GO TO HELL

To the seventh hell and back
I love you with all my demons
Bowing to your every blink
Until you do no more.

The profane words of the chime
Scorned by the acoustic guitar
You fuck up my mind to bits
With love and vigilance.

I abhor all your living organs
Beating with a love not mine
Then I absolve your selfishness
To mollify what's left of a broken pulse.

And the monitor beeps
With every one of my heartbeats
I let my soul purge, and I urge it
To penetrate you.

A straight line. A long beep.
Straight to hell, inside you.
Witnessing the deceit... Oh, your eyes!
Now see through another.

CONFESSION

Your whitewashed eyes reflect upon the mirror of a knife
Pretty as a rainbow on a rainy cold day,
Where you get all muddy and filthy...
You look at the sun and can't appreciate it less
And as you sit by the window, the candle burns
The rainbow struggles to keep itself in place
You look at it, with your twinkly eyes,
Then you turn your head to look at the clouds
Those heavy with rain.
The colorful arch loses its chance, fades away
With your bright eyes looking elsewhere
The knife stares at me,
As I look at your steely eyes once more
Wide open they are, so brown they are
So scared I am, I'm sure I didn't!
Recalling zero memories, wanting to know nothing,
I walk to the window where you were standing
The candle is dead, I look at the red
You meant the world to me...
I'm on my own now; I didn't do it, though!
You did it to torture me, but do I care?
The sun is coming out, as shy as a mouse
It reflects upon the knife, right into my eyes; it blinds me
I know nothing, heard nothing, saw nothing
But the knife now knows it all...
I bury it in the mud you ruined my favorite carpet with
And fix your face to the wall
So you can stare at me no more!

LAMENT

Regrets, Thursday at 11:20 pm
As we—shockingly—watch a gem
Wither.
We've taken it for granted
Ever since it all started
Never
Seeing that we're fooled
To put our faith in this world;
Not so clever!
But you won't be there on Eids
They say you're there with your deeds
But it differs.
Can't you see? Haven't you learned?
Oh humans, what have you earned?
Not a thing.
One, two, three trillion? A zillion?
Your blood vermilion?
Whatever.
There comes a day when you go
And life does not cease to flow
We shiver.
Because by the end of May,
You'll be on your way…
Tears, a river.
And we'll bid farewell to your power
And on your stone leave a flower
Love severs
Our hearts, leaving them in flames
Our cries, nothing tames…
Don't
Leave
Just
Yet.
Don't
Leave,
Ever!

UNKNOWN

Lurking in the shadow
You see the nightlight
Believing it's your safe haven
Living in denial
Caused by not knowing.
You, poor soul
Standing tall, so hollow
Your passions out of sight
The croaking calls of a raven
Lead your mind to the trial
The fatal ideas flowing
Sucking your life into a black hole
Glaring into emptiness, how shallow
Your body eaten up by fright
The road toward oblivion you're paving
In a world gone vile
Where our scars are glowing
Reminding us that it's all out of control.

A wish gone far
Wished upon a deranged falling star
That's exactly what you are.

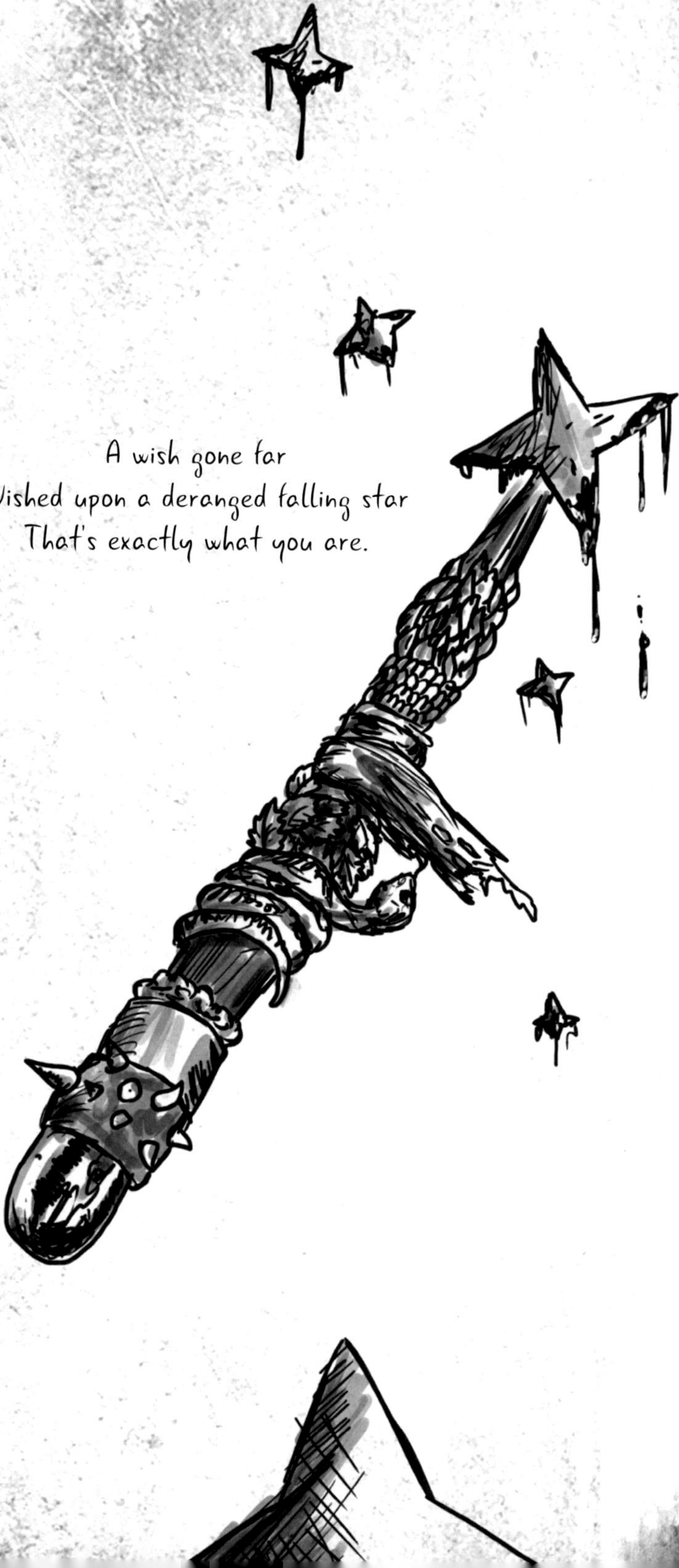

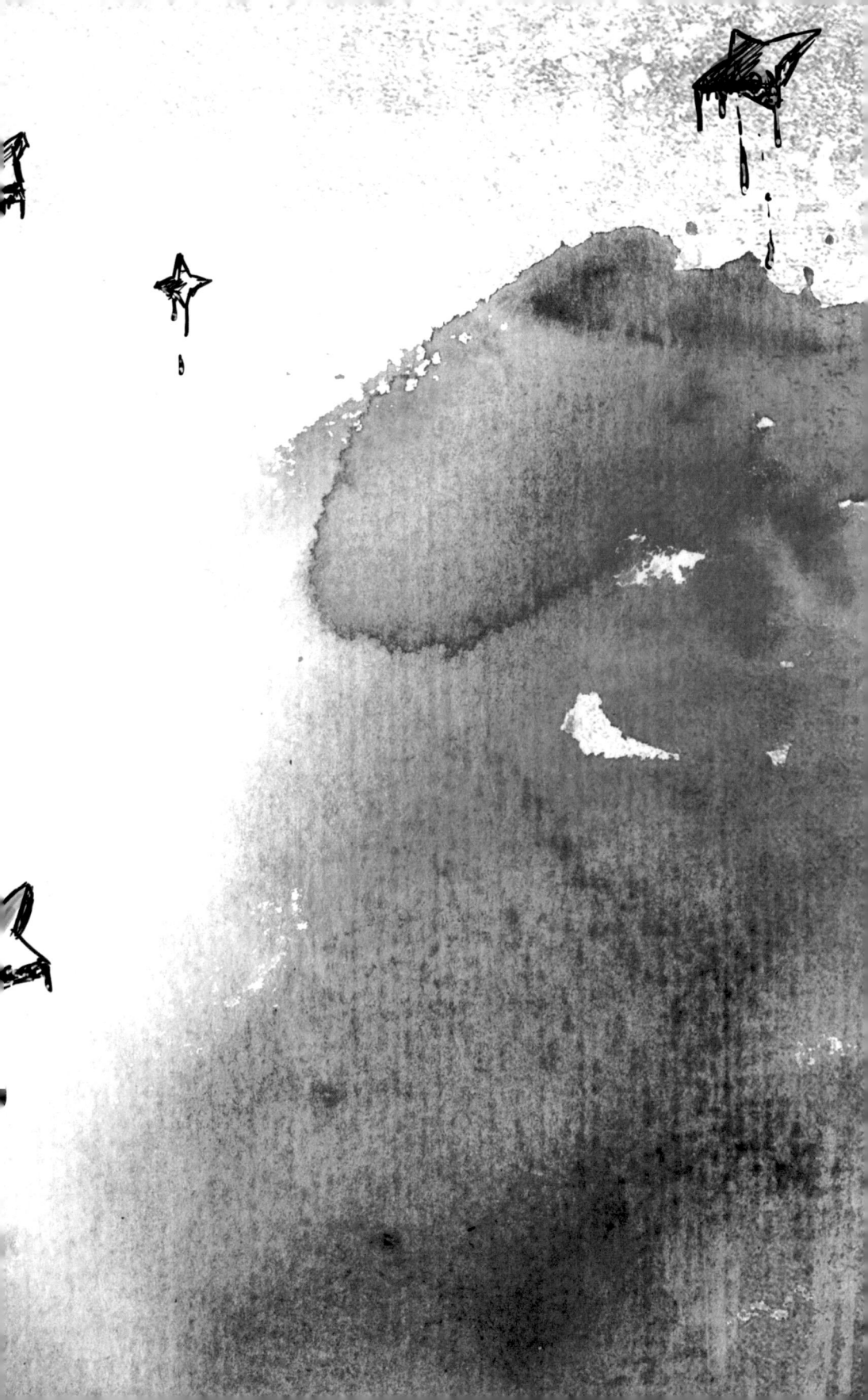

ONCE UPON A BROKEN RHYME

Answers hidden under piled-up memories
Yet questions were never asked
We could speak in song all day long
And feel it in our hearts, faking smiles
Hiding behind pierced wounds
That no words can ever mend
But at the end of the day, we'd know
And we'd shut our eyes, real tight
To dream, to never again remember
Yet once more, you go above and beyond
To put on a show, forcing me to let go
Of every-damned-thing... but the memory of you!

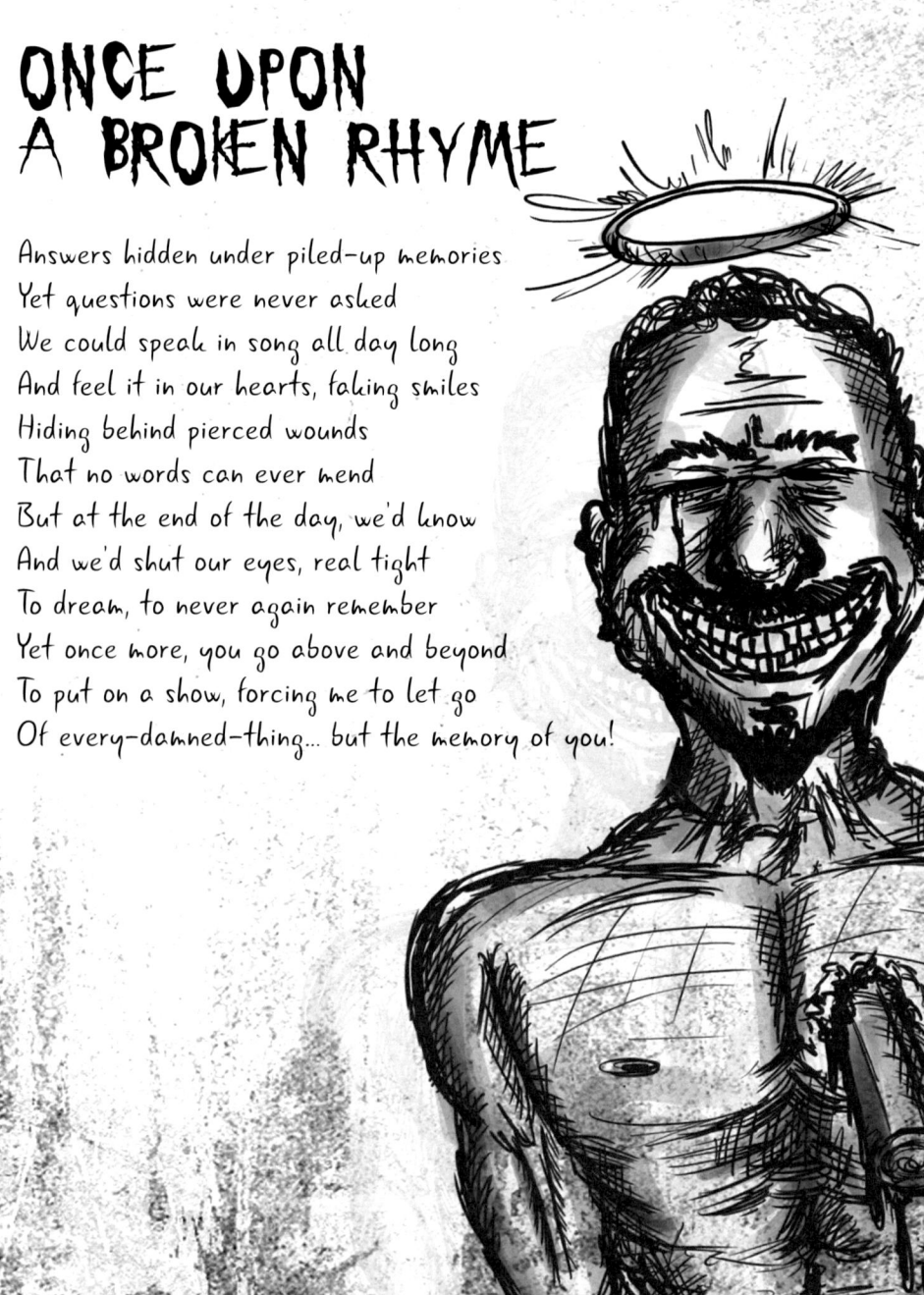

IN FLAMES

You promised me fire
Yet burned me with your cold
You breathed in my peace
Severing its final chord
You intruded into my existence
And watched me grow old
You lied to me in silence
Because words are just words
You spoke very little
But each time your cherry lips moved,
I realized that silence is mere gold.

SORRY?

Seeing bullets racing to the sky
For he who had a low soul
He promised our heart rhythm to unify
Till mine quivered out of control.

Thought my soft him would beautify
But I should've thought again
As his hard-heartedness did only nullify
My smile, my eyes, and joy it did detain.

I begged my tears never to leave my eye
But they double-screwed me
He did not even bother to justify
That was my worth to him apparently.

His entourage would always glorify
What they never got to eyewitness
His warmth and fragility terrify, petrify,
Terrorize my senses to sickness.

But I cherish him, that won't just die
And as he pierces my brain with deceit
For reasons I did not know why
He asks me...
All his doings from my memory to delete.

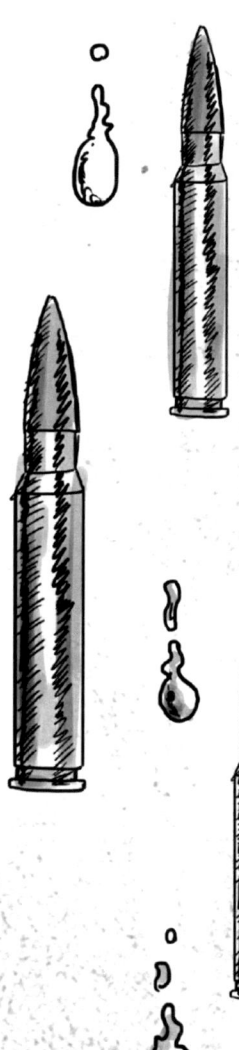

WORDLESS

Reminiscences of us...
"Sitting on the sidewalk,
Carving our names on the 2-feet-long wall
Dying the pavement white with dust
Marking our presence there,
In a place ours no more.
We inherit the burden, the dust in our lungs,
And leave the cherries to be harvested by the witty.
Memories of hurt limbs,
Of unfinished conversations,
Of disappointed brain cells
Linger there, long enough for one to realize
The dream has got real,
The wounded mind is remedied,
The confusion is undraped,
And the people are long lost."
...have got me nowhere.

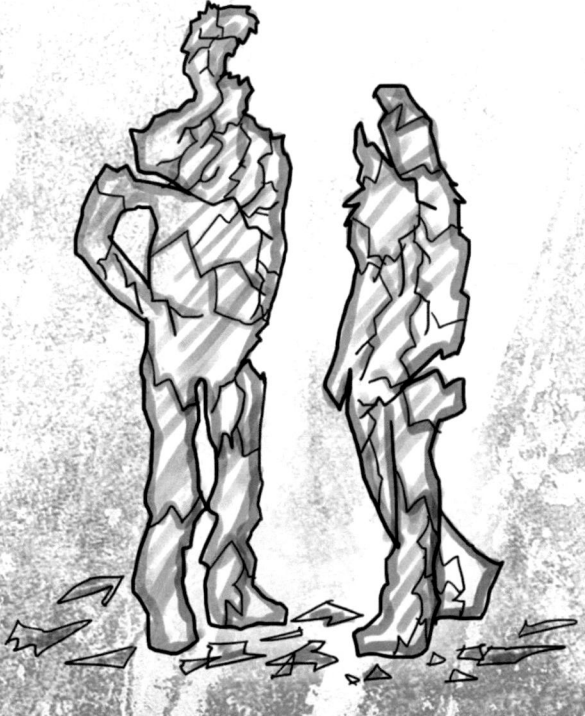

THE FRAME

The flashy flowery frame
The wide, pretty smile
That speaks a thousand languages...
A mind captured by a click
Sometimes better mortalized!
Behind that smile
Lies a deadly poisoned thought
A rotten philosophy
Hides behind prettiness
Kidnapped by a flash
That moves forward,
Or backward...
CLICK
You are turned inanimate.

KILLED

Eyes strictly pale
Drizzly only when the sound
Comes out of the light...
What is becoming of me?
A dead figure floating
An illusion created by man
Aiming at a wretched soul.
A cemetery is at an advantage
For death is inevitable
So obvious to those who live
So obnoxious to those alive...
Man lives, thinking he rules the game
Game is there to prove him mortal.
Yes, melancholic and hollow
Since you started to become real.

THE MIST

When the cradle rocks, forward and back
Mind is empty, empty is jolly
When Sun starts setting bashfully
Colorful nights and rich days follow its track
As those elapse, Sun cries for forgiveness
But the boy grows a mustache
Parents—the inevitable clash
Creativity stumbles upon the abyss
When Sun is murdered, it's time to rebel
Seriousness gets edible; man fills his mouth with rubbish
Rise up, fellow, revolt against the snobbish
Become part of who they are, or stand still
A mad man, a loner among his gang
Mind is so full, empty is fatality
Filling with meaninglessness the casualty
Proud of the rosy wall where his certificates hang.

GREY SUN

When the grey sun rose at night
You were all bothered and uptight
Nothingness filled your space
Putting an end to the land of grace
'As long as it rises late at night you see,
Why don't we call it moon and end this misery?'
You were so threatened by the change
That you couldn't believe in anything strange
Thus, you cut the speaker's head
And spread rumors about things kept unsaid
Propagandas were born on the bed of truth
To a mother that was slain in her youth
And a father who has been sitting for a long time
'Enough?' The thought was simply a crime
That no answer ever echoed in the cosmos
And grey rays were all that followed
Yet, you were still sitting, not moving a limb
For you, it started to get gloomy and grim...
So here is what happened eventually
(Or did not actually...)
The sitting man fell off the chair one day
Buried under the chair, or so they say
They became one; and as he lay
His bones were fed by the grey rays.

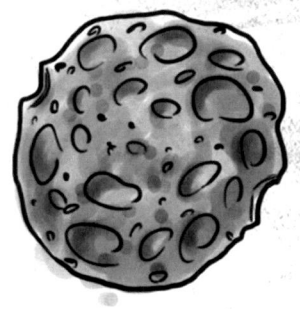

I stare into the mirror,
and all I see is glass,
with the reflection of a broken soul.

WHO DIED AND MADE HER KING?

The *she* inside my mind
Has been trying to take over
And for so long, I had the power to shut *her* up
And bury *her* between my worries.
Except that these days
I've grown weak in my brain
That she could dig up *her* beliefs
And plant them among my ideas.
Now, all I anticipate is the nothingness
Coming out of waiting.
All means nothing
Even happiness.
To her, waiting is the only option.
Waiting is joy!
But for what?
For the darkness of night
That with it comes sleep.
Sleep...
Through which I live my reality and *hers*.

A SPIDER WEB?

The oak tree gazed deeply into my eyes
As if realizing its thousand-year-old branches
Grew out of my skin.
I then sat under it
But its disgust of me started growing
As I started rotting.
I raised my head in agony
Or remorse
For standing face-to-face with it for so long
Without understanding the relationship
Springing out of the torn cobweb
Dying between its leaves.

With every spider web woven comes life.
But no, it's the other way around
Life is a spider web;
You either cut your way through it
Or get stuck and never get out.
That was the moral spinning in my head
When I woke up suffering from sunstroke.

BREAKABLE

A leaking sky
A spiral-patterned umbrella
The safest doors,
Unbreakable
Yet so breakable.

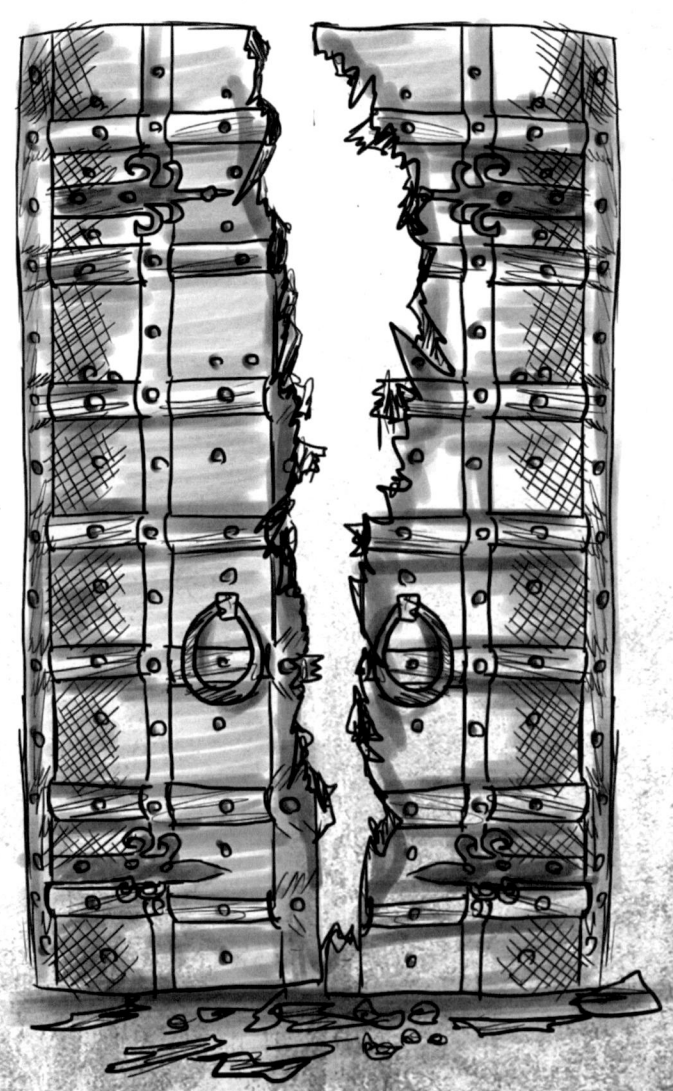

BREAKABLE TOO

Iris dry,
Sky starless
Heartless, you cry
Sigh, I'm breathless
Fruitless is your lie
Rely on how I'm careless
Faceless, I'll get by
I loathe your selfishness, you faithless
Remorseless was I
Why did you turn worthless?

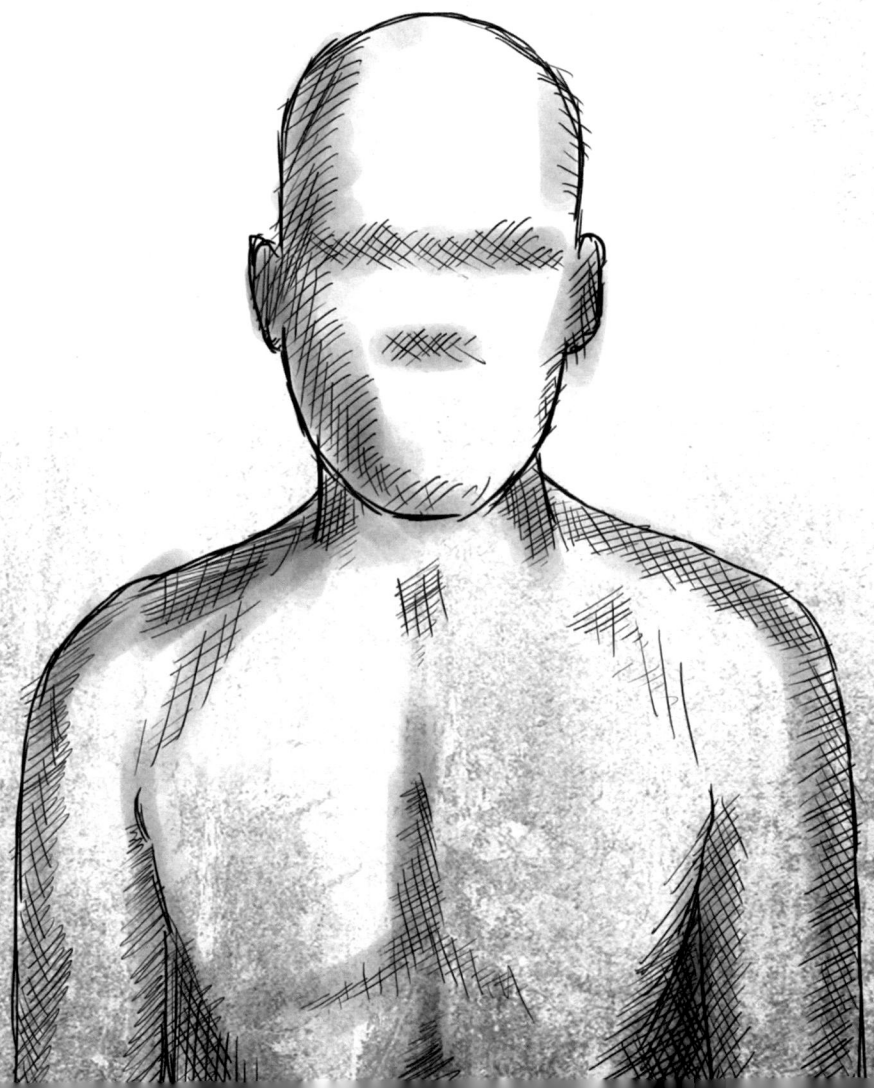

IDEALISM

In reality, we've met
A first look is all it took
Haven't talked through it yet
We're only two characters
Lost in-between a million-paged book
Having seen you in a dream or has it been real?
I can't tell...
I bet you can't say how you feel
Even now when the book came to an end,
And we got imprisoned by computer cells
Lonely amongst the crowds
Being set free by your presence
A life revolving around making you proud
Eventually lost its essence
No, it hasn't lost its real core
You are my elixir of life
Can't get enough; always need more
Being with you amuses me better than a soldier playing the fife
Sighs... adolescence is considered a magical episode
But days do pass and draw a conclusion
Mine crossed fields and deserts, and mountains they climbed

To get to the point that you have been a delusion
A figment of my imagination
Back then, you were the reason that kept my soul inside
Now I'm mature enough to know that it is not sufficient
An unarranged meeting has started a conflict
Does this ring a bell?
You've followed your instinct,
You're not blamed nor was it efficient
A bad choice of time, or maybe person
I couldn't get it at the right time
It's suicidal drinking its poison
It's a sin; it's a crime
I spat the poison and walked away
And this is what Plato called the ideal state!
Truth hurts, I'm still an adolescent and it's my day
You still have to answer the question, and I still have to wait
Two diverging ways we'll have to cross:
We either stay and pour our hearts out,
Or we move on and never feel bad for the loss
I'd say the answer feeling no remorse, no doubt:
Sorry, Plato, there's no such thing as an ideal state!

CUPID'S DART

Toward the light I march
As it is still dark in here
It's only the start.

I choose to march, this time
For all I used to fear
Was what's in your heart.

So I march, in no direction
Aiming for a destination
That will set us apart.

And I still march, nonetheless
As if it was a role-play
And I was stealing your part.

Toward darkness I march
With proud steps
Since Cupid's reclaimed his dart.

HAVE FAITH

It all began
With a leap of faith
When a heart fluttered
Raced, pounded
Until crushed
And again
I took a leap
This time down from the edge
Into the abyss
And I befriended my demons
And darkness became our playground
Gloom, our philosophy
Till one day, the sun,
Dull no more, blue no more
Spoke to me and said,
"Look before you leap."

FREE BELIEF

An ultimate reality, shattered
Not a matter of "appearances"
But of "reality"
Contrary to decency
Incivility is the course of nature
Quite a catch, yet lacking graciousness
A quality acquired, not born
And rarely found
Unless one wants to inhale,
The rainbow appears, then the spider web
Same happens with one sip,
Although it's coarseness to do it,
He who does it pays the price of losing it.

ONLY YOU

I bury myself in a reality, not mine
And when I dream (I do)
I fall into your trap, every time
Obsession feasts on a memory
A glance, your voice
Fantasizing, recalling a nightmare
That now sounds euphoric
Feels heart-warming
Stirs my weaknesses
Forces tears, no years
To wash away brilliant regrets
And whenever you crush me again
I shut my eyes, terminate my sight
Better judgment fades
Gets sucked into your world
My downfall, yet I dream
(Yes, I do).

IDENTITY

Mine is taken while his is falsified
My honor; a just cause
In a world that once told me
I was free
Then stole my culture
Changed my name
Ripped me off my identity
Put me in a trance
With an unending arrow
That goes down, down to the ground!
He doesn't know who I really am
Been standing since the days of Adam
He cannot break me
For I have no expectations at all...
I was promised to settle one day
Eventually, he dies, I belong
A vision
Soon to be transformed into a reality.

TO LET GO

I tightly close my eyes
To hear my screaming inside
It's time for the final goodbye
'Cause I can't anymore hide.

I trusted you
Only hurt myself
I believed in you
Only hurt myself
I loved you
Only hurt myself.

No remorse, no more lies
No compromises; the real objection
I strip off all masks, all disguise
To only see my true reflection.

I trusted you
I forgive myself
I believed in you
I forgive myself
I loved you
I forgive myself.

And the affection turns into an infection
I'll always have myself, what have you got?
I hear you speak with no inflection
Knowing that without me, you have naught!

I trusted you
Nevermore
I believed in you
Nevermore
I loved you
Never, nevermore.

WHEN I CLOSE MY EYES

What is a dream
But a mirror to the mind's eye
And all I can see
Is your reflection
Fixed, in every scene
With every other thing
Simply changeable
Merely floating
Leaving no trace of memory
In a mind, a disappointing maze
Where only you know the way
To the nonsense we call a dream.

ANXIETY RULES

They just came sneaking
Thoughts dismissed
Incomplete ideas
About one controversial issue.
They kept creeping, crawling in her head
She did her best to let go of the pain, the fear
Standing alone on the edge is a tough thing to deal with
She closed her eyes to lift her soul
It was then when she realized that it was taken.
She got past the boulevard of bafflement
Expecting to vanish
It only urged her to become more anxious
In a place where there're so many winning causes
But it's just too late when she figured out that's not it
It's not them!
They are neither an illusion nor a myth
She's not imaginary
Although it's all about sensationalism!
How come she walked down the street all screaming
She sure expected them to be different
In her fantasy world.
Dear,
Welcome to the existent world
Where they are true
Where they can be honest and sincere
Sorry, they fooled you at that time
It was easy to take advantage of you.
Indeed...
Fearful you will never make it to the finish line.

A FLARE OF REALITY

Stripping off the remorse I've felt with every drop of acid pumping into my stomach, and washing away the tears I shed feeling like a schmuck... I never heard your voice.

In a classroom-like hall, I fantasized a 6-year-old's confession, of things so true, so vivid. Of things fabricated... but I never felt whole.

I raise my hand to reach you. But the long distance, the coldness, and the fear hinder me. And when I dare my fingers to caress your face, I get so close, I touch the air.

Throwing a flower into the oasis turns it into a rock. Yet, you threw me a rose, and I ran after you. And when you got home, you shut the door.

Never getting it, forever demanding the best in everyone, I felt my feet growing heavier. I moved them with force, till I got to the door. I threw my fist on the rotten wood, and knocked, and knocked.

And the door fell to the ground, crashed and broke into smithereens. It was unlocked, but my fist did not realize it. It was hanging in the empty space, and I covered my face, wishing it was a dream.

Uncovering my eyes, hands so bare, I glared through obscurity. My eyes turned into two tiny red globes. Filled with water, my irises finally beheld reality.

THE REST IS YET TO COME

If I could go back in time
I would suppress my rhyme
I would gaze at the stars more often
And my heart I would soften
I would not seek perfection
Nor everyone's affection
I would live more freely
And much less ideally
I would not let reality mess with my head
My imagination would be my sanctuary instead
I would embrace my flaws
And dare to break some laws
I would not let anyone near my heart
Or allow them in my life to take part
I would not dream any dream
And my soul I would redeem
By seizing the day, the moment
And not defining myself by cement
I would belong to the place I'm in
Not to the land that has my kin
But time is not a toy
Even if my watch I destroy
It will get me first, that's for sure
This shithole of a life I'll have to endure
My choices, I'll have to suffer the consequence
Live, rot, and enjoy the nonsense.

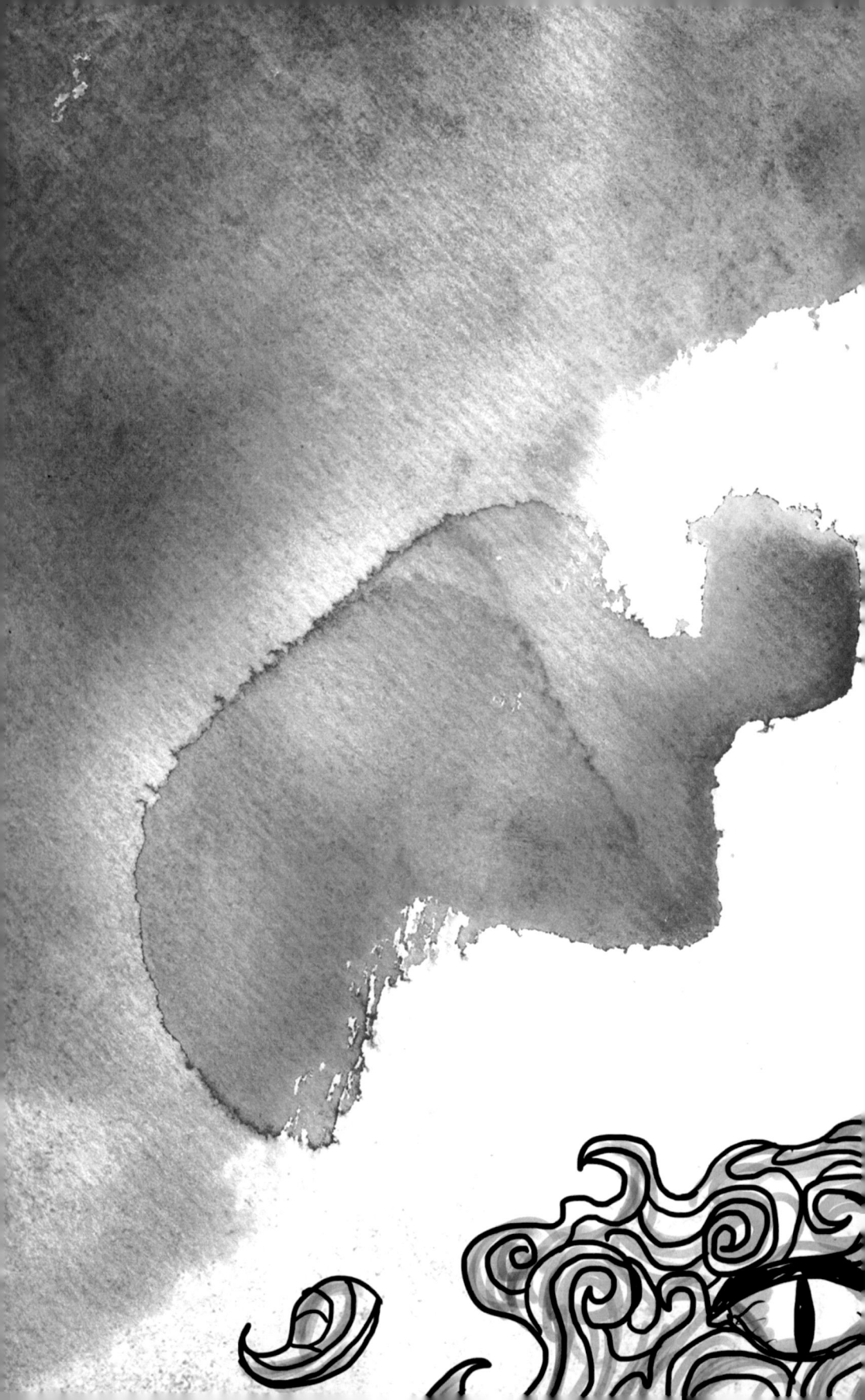

My conscience weaves clouds
To cage it, keeping down its loud
A smirk, it walks free and proud.

WHITE

Clouds fall up and down,
Disintegrate, vanish
As my tears abandon my tear duct,
Be it black iris, grey iris,
You are going to hear me cry.

My inside anticipates a clown,
Knowing they can be too clannish
I'm not excelling my code of conduct.
To the world I'm a slow virus,
Spreading in late July.

As the train pauses, the renown
The anti-humility, very mannish
That my courage I plucked,
In my world I'm the main actress
And on my meekness I rely.

Closing my eyes, touching my gown
Ideas evaporate, I banish
My entity, I need to reconstruct
Of escapism, I'm desirous...
This is what I wanted my letter to imply.

LAVA

I, a volcano,
Erupting at any second,
"Doesn't have the motive," they'd say
I am unable to blow my top
"Doesn't have the heart," they'd cry
The lava burns my guts,
I need to go off!
As my inside burns, I look around,
Red-eyed, flaming
My mind yells, struggles,
My lava shudders,
Sneaks through my veins,
Disintegrating the stones within me
Awakening my lust for exploding...
In spite of it all,
I see the rainbow, and then,
Swallow the uprising lava
Hold it back,
Allowing my body to melt gradually.

THE STORY OF QUITE A KNIGHT

A figure I was following that night
Holding a pen, he thought he might
Build a bridge over the well of white.
A brick he drew, the glorious sight
Of a bridge built over a well so bright
Tie brick on brick with a rope so tight
For the man I stalked, it felt so right
He walked on the dust, on the ink, in spite
Of the fact that I did write
To warn him, yet he expressed his delight
And began to recite
The story of a child with a magic kite
That got the world to reunite
Although suffering from plight...
Our hero believed the well was his by birthright
Until one day, a strong red light
Came out, erased the ink, and swallowed the knight
Taking him down to zero height
He tried to draw a ladder, feeling so uptight
The well took hold of his pen, leaving his contrite
Heart burning with a slight
Mite of aching, unfortunate fright.

"D" LUCK

Dreaming of green tears impinging upon my thoughts,
I wake up to realize that a dream is not a dream.
So in memory of all that is good, I pray,
I look high to realize it did not last long enough.
To remember how long ago it was, I had to disable my guts;
My lungs froze and my heart raced like never before.
And what a rhythm!
I can't see you in the morning light,
And when the nocturnal hour encircles emptiness
Day beseeches mercy, and death haunts the sunshine!
Thoughts of how I can't make it,
The dilemma of existence still remains.

THE SKY'S FAIRYTALE

My eyes wandered. Yet, they found nothing worth looking at. But, there was something so magical, so out of this world, right there where I never looked. It stood with pride, in extreme brilliance. It shone, sparkled with every possible hue. It took my breath away as it showed me its essence. Illuminating dots flashed like diamonds reflecting the light of love. A moment in time turned me around, mirroring the best in me that I once thought I lost.

One look at the sky, and I was captivated forever. Now I know I need it. If down or upset, or even when my madness starts throbbing, I gaze at the countless elements that generate its fashion. A blaze soothes my infinite anger, repressed. Unexpressed words of wonder draw a curve on my face.

This did happen once. I wouldn't lie to you about my one sky. But now it's grey. Grey when the sun's rage grew more intense, when the moon got much brighter to prevent me from sleeping. It's all about confusion. Crystal-clear is nonsense, a fairytale. Oh, how I loathe fairytales!

My sky has turned against me. First time, it ignored my glances. It turned grey when all I offered was a rainbow. The time after, it shocked me with a thunderbolt, leaving me a skeleton, with a halo fading away, getting one step closer to death every single moment.

Sky, I'm again in need of you.

A MEMORY

Physically tired,
Emotionally devastated,
I remember the old days
When things were fine,
When the world was pure,
When the blackness of the world
Was still an enigma.
I remember you,
And the world you built me.
I recall the words you shared with me.
I remember the secret windows you opened,
The original doors,
The cupholders...
Then I pass out.

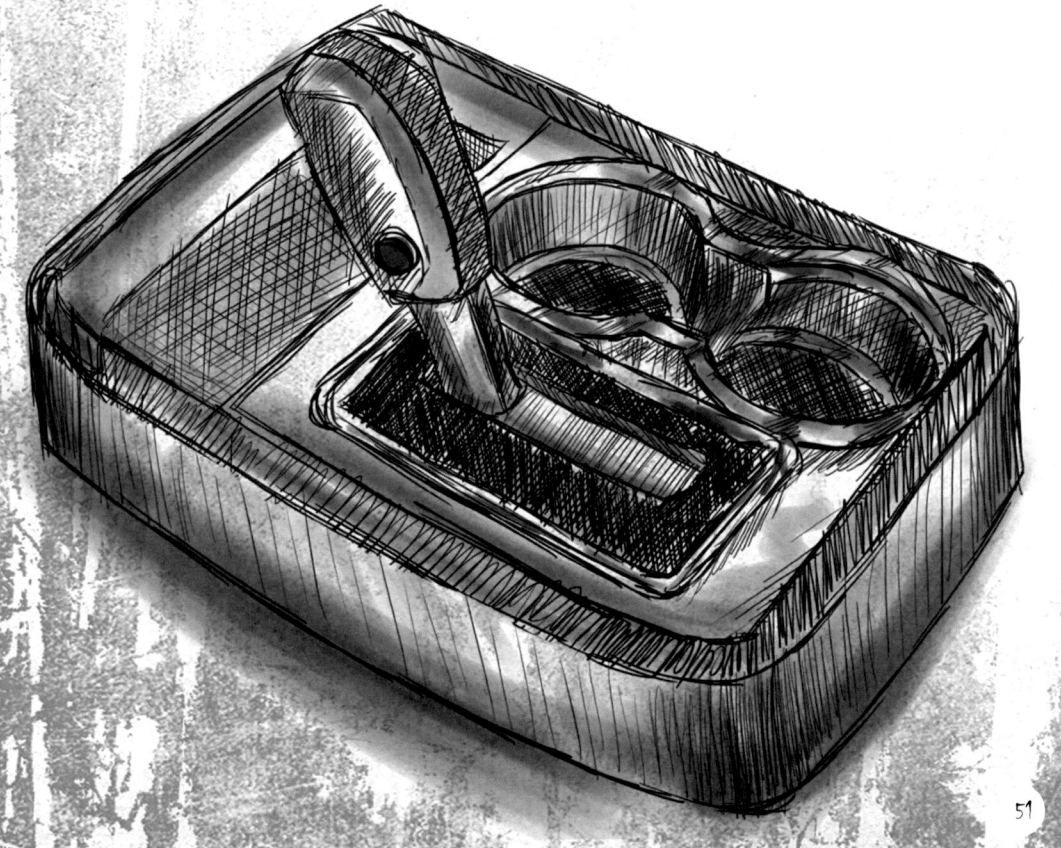

SLEEPLESSNESS

Darkness takes place
When the two silver dots stop shining, drawing
A smile of somber on the slumbering vagabond's face,
And the road of the dying man is drifting.
The ringing bells drive me into sleeplessness.
Clouds change the color of the dome,
And stars wipe away all the vagueness
Provoked by the fountain's foam.
Thinking of tomorrow, I grow anxious
And when I sleep, I dream of you…
A fantasy of rigid people, yet gracious
What an attitude I've gotten myself into.
When darkness takes place, the moon rises
But the sun sinks into nowhere.
Fact after fact, man watches
And believes… and no one would dare
To go against the flow, against the herds
Because then, and only then the voices echo again.
Sleeplessness, no more sounds of birds,
All that you get is the ringing bell and rain.
When darkness takes place today,
As any other day, there will be misery,
Charming despair, and a desperate hurray.
At that moment, I close the drapes and go to sleep.

TO THOSE WHO CARE...

Why would we worry
When living is a cliché?
We never say we're sorry
Instead we say "touché".

Faces of beauty,
Beautiful faces,
Acknowledge your duty
That soon death displaces.

Smithereens of shattered glass scattered
Marking the street a dancing floor.

Confusion is a state of denial
When "going" is inescapable
Accepting is a trial
Of which not everyone is capable.

Unleash your soul, permit it to float
High, high where your gestures wear off
Light the sky and evil promote
As all you did was play tough.

Smithereens of shattered glass scattered
Marking the street a dancing floor.

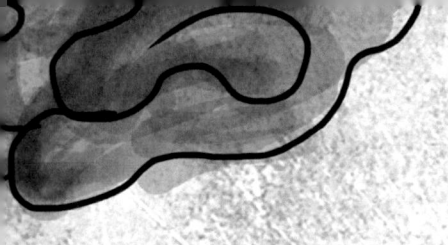
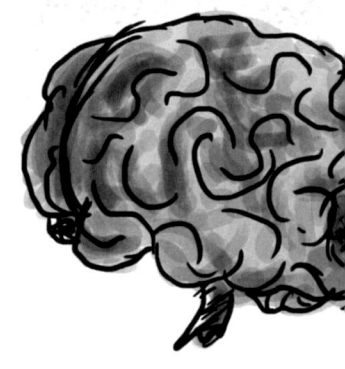

I thought I had it all
Until I realized that all is what falls behind
Leaving me empty-handed,
Empty-minded!

THE HOUSE OF DOOM

I salute you in the house of doom,
Where the ground grows special creatures
To cause the decay of the tiles...
The house of doom,
Where the paint climbing up the wall,
Causes the disintegration of the roof...
Reaching the clouds,
Creating a rainbow
So artificial.

INSIEME

IN NATURA

En 2021, Irina Rozovsky et Mark Steinmetz ont été invités en Italie pour réaliser un projet photographique; ils ont séjourné à Castelfranco Veneto en Vénétie et à Lecce dans les Pouilles. Le thème qui devait guider leur travail était la « nature » ; un thème aux déclinaisons multiples dans la représentation d'un paysage varié et inconstant comme celui d'aujourd'hui, qui se reflète sans cesse dans nos existences en conditionnant également notre manière d'observer la réalité.

Ce volume rassemble une sélection de photographies réalisées par les deux artistes dans deux régions géographiques éloignées l'une de l'autre. Des lieux où la nature se manifeste sous des formes expressives différentes et où la relation entre corps et espace semble assumer, à travers la combinaison de l'ombre et de la lumière, des valeurs aléatoires, parfois absolues.

Insieme (ensemble) est l'interprétation d'une expérience photographique italienne composée comme un journal intime. Proposant un double regard qui tisse délicatement la trame narrative, les photographies de Rozovsky et Steinmetz se côtoient et se succèdent, alternent et se répondent selon un rythme discontinu et fluctuant, comme les épisodes de la vie. Tendant à saisir des événements imprévus et des rencontres singulières, mais surtout les instants d'un quotidien vécu ensemble, les images dénotent une familiarité particulière avec les lieux traversés et en révèlent l'authenticité naturelle.

« Personne ne parvient à distinguer vraiment la fantaisie de la réalité – racontait Gianni Celati –, ensemble (*insieme*) elles forment une chose difficile à comprendre, mais elles sont une seule et même chose. (…) La distinction entre fantaisie et réalité est une superstition, qui empêche de penser et de 'sentir' les sentiments : les sentiments n'existent que comme états d'imagination.[1] » Pour Luigi Ghirri aussi la photographie est « un grand jouet magique qui parvient à conjuguer le grand et le petit, les illusions et la réalité, le temps et l'espace, notre conscience adulte et le monde enchanté de l'enfance[2] ».

Sur les traces d'une nature en mutation dans son devenir même, le travail de Rozovsky et Steinmetz traduit la vision d'une métaphore affective provenant d'une expérience familière partagée, perceptible dans un continuel jeu d'échos entre un regard et l'autre, un lieu et l'autre, entre micro et macro, entre le seuil de la réalité et celui de l'imagination.

---

1. M. Belpoliti, A. Stefi (dirigé par), *Gianni Celati. Il transito mite delle parole. Conversazioni e interviste 1974-2014*, Quodlibet, Macerata 2023, pp. 158-159, traduction de Lise Caillat.

2. P. Costantini, G. Chiaramonte (dirigé par), *Luigi Ghirri. Niente di antico sotto il sole. Scritti e immagini per un'autobiografia*, SEI, Turin 1997, p. 11, traduction de Lise Caillat.

In 2021, Irina Rozovsky and Mark Steinmetz were invited to take part in two photographic projects in Italy, one in Castelfranco Veneto (the Veneto region) and the other in Lecce (Puglia). The subject intended to drive the work was 'nature'; a word with so many variations of meaning in the context of today's diversified, fragmented landscape, which constantly reflects our lives as well as condition the way that we observe reality.

This book compiles a selection of the artists' photographs of these two Italian regions so far apart from one another. These are places where nature reveals itself through different forms of expression and where the relationship between body and space, captured in a combination of light and shade, seems to take on an inconsistent and sometimes absolute value.

Insieme (together) tells of a photographic experience in Italy that was composed in the form of an intimate, personal diary. With the artists' dual gaze gently organizing a narrative structure, Rozovsky and Steinmetz's photographs sit alongside one another, alternating and rotating in harmony with a discontinuous, fluctuating rhythm, just as in life's episodes. These pictures, which seem almost poised to capture unexpected events and unusual encounters but especially moments of a shared daily life, express a singular familiarity with the places being found, conveying the natural character of their authenticity.

As Gianni Celati wrote, "No-one really manages to distinguish fantasy from reality – together (*insieme*) they are difficult to understand, but they are a single entity [...] The difference between fantasy and reality is superstition, in other words something that prevents you from thinking and "feeling" feelings. Feelings only exist as imaginary states."[1] Luigi Ghirri also regarded photography as a "huge magic toy that succeeds in linking the large and the small, illusions and reality, time and space, our awareness as adults and the fairy-tale world of our childhood."[2]

Following the traces of a nature that mutates in the very process of self-creation, Rozovsky and Steinmetz's work expresses a visual metaphor drawn from a shared family experience, one that can be seen in an unending game of give and take, from one gaze to the other, from the micro to the macro, from one place to the next, between the thresholds of reality and the imaginary.

---

1. M. Belpoliti, A. Stefi (ed.), *Gianni Celati. Il transito mite delle parole. Conversazioni e interviste 1974-2014*, Quodlibet, Macerata 2023, pp. 158-159, translation by Gray Sutherland.

2. P. Costantini, G. Chiaramonte (ed.), *Luigi Ghirri. Niente di antico sotto il sole. Scritti e immagini per un'autobiografia*, SEI, Torino 1997, p. 11, translation by Gray Sutherland.

INSIEME
Irina Rozovsky, Mark Steinmetz

Première édition publiée par
First edition published by
Prima edizione pubblicata da
Chose Commune & OMNE

Photographies
Photographs
Fotografie
Irina Rozovsky, Mark Steinmetz

Texte
Text
Testo
Stefania Rössl

Direction éditoriale
Editorial direction
Direzione editoriale
Cécile Poimbœuf-Koizumi,
Stefania Rössl, Massimo Sordi

Conception graphique
Graphic design
Progetto grafico
Damiano Fraccaro / Otium

Traduction anglaise
English Translation
Traduzioni in lingua inglese
Gray Sutherland

Traduction française
French translation
Traduzioni in lingua francese
Lise Caillat

Relecture
Proofreading
Revisione testi
Poppy Beale-Collins, Cécile Poimbœuf-Koizumi

Photogravure, impression et reliure
Colour separation, printing and binding
Prestampa, stampa e rilegatura
Grafiche Antiga Spa

Imprimé en Italie, août 2023
Printed in Italy, August 2023
Stampato in Italia, agosto 2023

ISBN: 979-10-96383-39-9
Achevé d'imprimer en août 2023
sur les presses de Grafiche Antiga
Dépôt légal 3e trimestre 2023

Pour cette édition
For this edition
Per questa edizione
© Chose Commune, 2023
© OMNE, 2023

Pour le texte
For the text
Per il testo
© Stefania Rössl, 2023

Pour les photographies en couleur
For the colour photographs
Per le fotografie a colori
© 2021 Irina Rozovsky

Pour les photographies en noir et blanc
For the black and white photographs
Per le fototografie in bianco e nero
© 2021 Mark Steinmetz

Pour l'écriture à la main en couverture
For the cover handwriting
Per la scrittura a mano in copertina
© 2023 Amelia Steinmetz

Chose Commune
studio@chosecommune.com
www.chosecommune.com

32 rue de Bruys
13005 Marseille
France

—

This book was published
on the occasion of the OMNEFEST 2023

INSIEME
Irina Rozovsky, Mark Steinmetz
Museo Casa Giorgione,
Castelfranco Veneto – TV, Italy
22 September – 29 October 2023

Curated by
Stefania Rössl, Massimo Sordi
Within the project
OMNE + TRANSIZIONI
Photographic campaign NATURE
(Castelfranco Veneto and Lecce,
September 2021)

www.o-m-n-e.com

Nel 2021 Irina Rozovsky e Mark Steinmetz sono stati invitati in Italia per una campagna fotografica soggiornando in Veneto e in Puglia, nelle città di Castelfranco Veneto e Lecce. Il tema che avrebbe guidato lo sviluppo del loro lavoro era "natura", termine che trova molteplici declinazioni nell'immagine di un paesaggio variegato e discontinuo, come quello contemporaneo, che si riflette costantemente nelle nostre esistenze condizionandone anche il modo di osservare la realtà.

Il volume raccoglie una selezione di fotografie eseguite dai due autori in due regioni geografiche distanti tra loro. Si tratta di luoghi in cui la natura si manifesta attraverso forme espressive differenti e dove la relazione tra corpo e spazio, attraverso il combinarsi della luce e dell'ombra, sembra assumere valenze mutevoli, talvolta assolute.

Insieme interpreta il racconto di un'esperienza fotografica italiana composta in forma di diario intimo e personale. Avvalendosi di un doppio sguardo, che delicatamente ne ordisce la struttura narrativa, le fotografie di Rozovsky e Steinmetz si accostano e si succedono, si alternano e si avvicendano secondo un ritmo discontinuo e fluttuante, così come gli episodi della vita. Pronte a cogliere accadimenti improvvisi e incontri singolari, ma specialmente istanti di un quotidiano vissuto insieme, le immagini esprimono una particolare familiarità con i luoghi incontrati trasmettendone un naturale carattere di autenticità.

"Nessuno riesce a distinguere veramente la fantasia dalla realtà – raccontava Gianni Celati – *insieme* sono una cosa difficile da capire, ma sono una cosa sola (...) La distinzione tra fantasia e realtà è una superstizione, cioè è qualcosa che impedisce di pensare e impedisce di 'sentire' i sentimenti: i sentimenti non esistono se non come stati d'immaginazione"[1]. Anche Luigi Ghirri pensava alla fotografia come "un grande giocattolo magico che riesce a coniugare il grande e il piccolo, le illusioni e la realtà, il tempo e lo spazio, la nostra adulta consapevolezza ed il fiabesco mondo dell'infanzia"[2].

Immergendosi nella dimensione di una natura plurale, che muta nel suo stesso farsi, il lavoro di Irina Rozovsky e Mark Steinmetz esprime la visione di una metafora affettiva tratta da un'esperienza famigliare condivisa, percettibile in un gioco continuo di rimandi, da uno sguardo e all'altro, dal micro al macro, da un luogo all'altro, tra soglie di realtà e immaginazione.

---

[1] M. Belpoliti, A. Stefi (a cura di), *Gianni Celati. Il transito mite delle parole. Conversazioni e interviste 1974-2014*, Quodlibet, Macerata 2023, pp. 158-159.

[2] P. Costantini, G. Chiaramonte (a cura di), *Luigi Ghirri. Niente di antico sotto il sole. Scritti e immagini per un'autobiografia*, SEI, Torino 1997, p. 11.